10 minute

NO-BAKE MAKES

Annalees Lim

WAYLAND

First published in Great Britain in 2015 by Wayland

Copyright © Wayland, 2015

Dewey Number: 641.5'123-dc23
ISBN: 978 0 7502 8442 4
Ebook ISBN: 978 0 7502 9411 9
10 9 8 7 6 5 4 3 2 1

Printed in China

FSC

Wayland
An imprint of
Hachette Children's Group
Part of Hodder & Stoughton
Carmelite House
50 Victoria Embankment
London EC4Y 0DZ

An Hachette UK Company
www.hachette.co.uk

www.hachettechildrens.co.uk

Editor: Elizabeth Brent
Food stylist: Annalees Lim
Designer: Elaine Wilkinson
Photographer: Simon Pask, N1 Studios

The website addresses (URLs) and QR codes included in this book
were valid at the time of going to press. However, it is possible that
contents or addresses may have changed since the publication of
this book. No responsibility for any such changes can be accepted
by either the author or the Publisher.

Picture acknowledgements:
All step-by-step craft photography: Simon Pask, N1 Studios;
images used throughout for creative graphics: Shutterstock

Contents

No-bake makes

Baking is a great way to make your own delicious cakes, biscuits and breads. This book is the perfect introduction to baking, and will show you fun and simple ways to make nine tasty treats without turning on an oven.

From delicious desserts to bite-sized biscuits, there is something here for anyone with a sweet tooth! If you are new to cooking, or just want to try something different, then this is a great first step into baking.

You won't need to use an oven, but for some recipes you will need to melt things, such as chocolate. You can ask an adult to help you use a microwave, or a bowl placed over a saucepan of hot water. Whichever method you use, always remember to take care when handling anything hot, and to make sure you don't let anything burn. You'll also need kitchen scales, to weigh out some of the ingredients.

Baking is lots of fun but you can easily get messy, with sticky fingers or flour-covered clothes. Protect your clothes by wearing an apron and remember to roll up your sleeves before you start. Surfaces can get dirty quickly, but you can always wash them down afterwards with a warm, soapy cloth. If you have long hair, tie it back, and always wash your hands before and after baking.

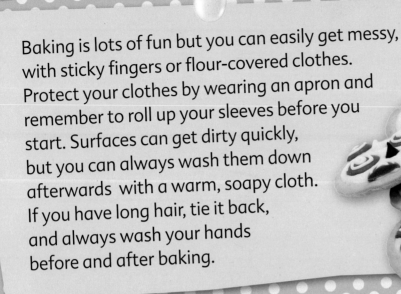

This book is just the start of your baking adventure! You can experiment by changing ingredients to make up your own recipes. It's up to you how you cook and create your dishes; recipes are there to be changed, so do things your own way.

Baking for yourself is always a fun way to pass the time, especially if it is dull and rainy outside — but the best part is sharing what you have made and seeing how much other people enjoy it! So what's stopping you? Stock up your baking cupboard, put on an apron and choose your own no-bake make to create.

Strawberries and cream cornflake cakes

Makes 12

These delicious cornflake cakes contain dried strawberries, making them perfect for a summer party!

1

Put the cake cases into the muffin tin.

2

Break the white chocolate into pieces in a large bowl, and melt it over a saucepan of hot water or using a microwave. Pour in a capful of vanilla extract and stir.

3

Mix in the cornflakes and dried strawberries, making sure everything is covered in chocolate.

4

Spoon the mixture into the cake cases.

5

Cut all four strawberry laces into three, and tie each part into a bow. Put a bow on top of every cornflake cake, then put them in the fridge to set.

Tip

Swap the berries for other dried fruit, such as cranberries (add orange extract instead of the vanilla extract), or cherries (add almond extract instead of vanilla to flavour).

Millionaires' biscuits

Makes 12

Millionaires' shortbread is always a favourite treat. Try making this version, using crushed digestive biscuits for the base.

You will need:

- 25 digestive biscuits
- 75g butter
- 1 tablespoon golden syrup
- 1 tin (approx 400g) caramel
- 200g milk chocolate

- A square or rectangular dish
- Greaseproof paper
- Scissors
- A sandwich bag
- A wooden spoon
- A rolling pin
- A large bowl
- A metal spoon
- A small bowl

1

Line the dish with greaseproof paper. Put the biscuits in the sandwich bag, and hit them gently with the back of the wooden spoon or a rolling pin to turn them into crumbs.

2

Melt 75g of butter in a large bowl, then tip in the crumbs and mix well.

3

Add the golden syrup to the crumb mix and then tip into the dish. Press down firmly with the back of a metal spoon.

4

Spread the caramel evenly over the biscuit base.

5

Melt the chocolate in a bowl, then pour it on top of the caramel. Put it in the fridge to set before cutting it into pieces.

Tip

If you gently shake the bag of biscuits, the larger pieces will rise to the top so you can easily see which bits still need to be made into crumbs.

Lemon meringue bites

Makes 6

You will need:

- 80g icing sugar
- 40g softened butter
- 12 mini meringues
- 3 teaspoons lemon curd
- 30g dark chocolate

- A small bowl
- A spoon
- A sandwich bag
- Scissors
- A chopping board or mat
- A wire cooling rack
- Greaseproof paper

These bite-sized meringues, filled with buttercream and lemon curd, make a delicious snack or gift.

1

Mix the icing sugar with the softened butter to make a stiff buttercream.

2

Put the mixture into the sandwich bag and cut off one corner. Pipe a swirl of buttercream onto six of the mini meringues.

3

Spoon half a teaspoon of lemon curd onto the six buttercream meringues.

4

Put the other six meringues on top of the lemon curd to make a sandwich. Place the meringue sandwiches onto a wire cooling rack, standing on top of some greaseproof paper.

5

Melt the dark chocolate and drizzle it over the meringue sandwiches. Leave until the chocolate has set.

Tip

Either soften your butter by keeping it out of the fridge or by putting it in a warm place like a windowsill or an airing cupboard. If you keep your butter in the fridge, then soften it slightly in a microwave before beginning.

Penguin fruit fondue

Makes 12

Grapes, covered in chocolate and decorated to look like penguins, are the ideal party food. Your guests will want to eat a whole flock of them!

Wash your grapes and stick two on each skewer.

Melt the dark chocolate in a bowl and dunk each of the skewers into it. Make sure you completely cover the grapes.

3

Turn the paper cup upside down and pierce the bottom with the skewers so they stand up.

4

Press two chocolate buttons into the wet chocolate and put the penguins in the fridge to set.

5

Use the icing pens to draw on an orange beak and feet, and black eyes and wings.

Tip

Explore making other fruity creatures! Try making rabbits using a strawberry for the face and a chocolate button, cut in half, for the ears.

Cake pop bites

Makes 12

Cake crumbs and frosting, moulded into balls and covered in chocolate and sprinkles, make cake pop bites – delicious mini-treats that are perfect as presents.

You will need:

- 200g Madeira cake
- 60g frosting
- 100g milk chocolate
- Sprinkles or chopped nuts

- A large bowl
- A spoon
- A chopping board or mat
- A small bowl
- A plate
- Paper cake cases

1

Put the cake in a bowl, and break it into crumbs.

2

Add the frosting and mix well, using your hands. You want it to be the consistency of Play-Doh, so you may need to add more cake crumbs or frosting.

3

Spoon a small amount of dark chocolate onto the peanut butter biscuits.

4

Scatter marshmallows and chocolate chips on top of the chocolate. Place the six plain biscuits on top of these.

5

Spread more chocolate on top of the biscuits and decorate with more marshmallows.

Tip

If you don't like peanut butter, you can make s'mores with jam, or even caramel.

Party popcorn

Party food doesn't get better than these crunchy popcorn slabs – mixed with chocolate, nuts and caramel sugar, they are ideal for snacking on!

You will need:

- 100g white chocolate
- 50g sweet popcorn
- 1/2 tablespoon golden syrup
- 1 tablespoon dark chocolate drops
- 1 tablespoon caramel sugar
- 1 tablespoon chopped nuts

- A small bowl
- A large bowl
- A spoon
- A chopping board or mat
- Greaseproof paper

1 Melt the white chocolate and mix it into the popcorn until it is all covered.

2 Add the golden syrup and mix well. The popcorn should be sticky, so you may need to add more syrup.

10 minute CRAFTS

Titles in the series:

SPRING
978 0 7502 8403 5

EASTER
978 0 7502 8194 2

NO-BAKE MAKES
978 0 7502 8442 4

SUMMER
978 0 7502 8330 4

MOTHER AND FATHERS DAY
978 0 7502 8196 6

ORIGAMI
978 0 7502 8445 5

AUTUMN
978 0 7502 8329 8

HALLOWEEN
978 0 7502 8195 9

DECORATIVE CARDS
978 0 7502 8444 8

WINTER
978 0 7502 8351 9

CHRISTMAS
978 0 7502 8172 0

JUNK MODELLING
978 0 7502 8443 1